To: ____

From: ____

"I wish for you a life of wealth, health and happiness; a life in which you give to yourself the gift of patience, the virtue of reason, the value of knowledge, and the influence of faith in your own ability to dream about and to achieve worthy rewards."

— *Jim Rohn*

Published by SUCCESS
200 Swisher Road
Lake Dallas, Texas 75065
Toll-free: 866-SUCCESS (782-2377)
www.SUCCESS.com

Printed in the United States of America.
Book design by Sam Watson and Floro Torres.
ISBN 978-1-935944-04-1

SPECIAL SALES

SUCCESS books are available at special discounts for bulk purchase for sales promotions and premiums. Special editions, including personalized covers, excerpts of existing books, and corporate imprints, can be created in large quantities for special needs. For more information, contact Special Markets, SUCCESS, sales@success.com.

THE JIM ROHN GUIDE TO PERSONAL DEVELOPMENT

➤ JIM ROHN ❮

For more than 40 years, Jim Rohn honed his craft like a skilled artist, helping people all over the world sculpt life strategies that expanded their imagination of what is possible. Jim set the standard for those who seek to teach and inspire others. He possessed the unique ability to bring extraordinary insights to ordinary principles and events. Those who had the privilege of hearing him speak can attest to the elegance and common sense in his material. It is no coincidence, then, that he is widely regarded as one of the most influential thinkers of our time and a national treasure. Jim authored numerous books and audio and video programs, and he helped motivate and shape an entire generation of personal development trainers and hundreds of executives from America's top corporations.

For additional information or to shop for Jim Rohn's best-selling books, CDs, DVDs and more, go to www.JimRohn.com.

➤ A NOTE ON THIS GUIDE ◄

The text of this pocket-size guide is based on transcripts of Jim Rohn's most popular lectures and writings on the subject of personal development. His original words have been transcribed, edited, rearranged and slightly modified in some instances for greater clarity.

As you read, you may recognize a familiar pace to the text. It is our hope that Jim's easy conversational tone and speaking style come across in your reading of each and every page. Though some of Jim's references may be out of date, his life philosophies and success principles transcend the years and are as relevant today as they were when he first expressed them.

The intent of this guide is to provide a concise, easy-to-read treatment of the subject matter that can be read in a short sitting of 15 to 20 minutes. Highlight your favorite parts and keep it close for easy reference again and again. Share it with friends, family, associates, clients and anyone you feel would benefit from the timeless wisdom of a true legend.

See page 48 for information on other booklets in the Jim Rohn Guide series.

THE JIM ROHN GUIDE TO PERSONAL DEVELOPMENT

One day my mentor, Mr. Earl Shoaff, said to me, "Jim, if you want to be wealthy and happy, learn this lesson well: Learn to work harder on yourself than you do on your job." I must admit that this was the most challenging assignment of all. This business of personal development lasts a lifetime.

You see, what you become is far more important than what you get. The important question to ask on the job is not, "What am I getting?" Instead, you should ask, "What am I becoming?" What you become directly influences what you get. Think of it this way: Most of what you have today, you have attracted by becoming the person you are today.

I've also found that income rarely exceeds personal development. Sometimes income takes a lucky jump, but unless you learn to handle the responsibilities that come with it, it will usually shrink back to the amount you can handle.

It is hard to keep that which has not been obtained through personal development. So here's the great axiom of life:

To have more than you've got, become more than you are.

SKILLS FOR SUCCESS IN THE MARKETPLACE

The marketplace is a demanding place. There is plenty of opportunity, but you've got to get ready for it and prepare for it. We've got to spend a portion of this year getting ready for next year, and we've got to spend a portion of this decade getting ready for the next decade. Hopefully the reason why we're here, looking well, doing fairly well, is because we spent a portion of the last decade getting ready for this decade.

So, a big share of life is spent getting ready, getting prepared, and part of it is the development of skills. I've got a good key phrase for you to start with in developing skills that make for success in the marketplace. First, it starts with personal development, self-improvement, making measurable progress.

PERSONAL DEVELOPMENT IS NOT AN EASY MATTER

Personal development is a push. It's a struggle. It's a challenge. There wouldn't be any winning without a challenge. That's what life is all about. It's the struggle and the challenge to develop ourselves and our skills to see what we can create in the way of value in the marketplace.

Life is all about creating skills and value and taking those skills and value to the marketplace and seeing what it will return for you. Now it also has a social part, a spiritual part as well as the physical part, and we're going to talk about some of those parts.

New habits don't come easy, but they can be developed. Sometimes when you develop a lot of momentum in one direction, it's not that easy to change but it is possible. It isn't easy, but it's possible. Somebody once said, success is 10 percent inspiration and 90 percent perspiration. You've just got to read the books, learn the skills, put yourself through the paces, do the mental pushups and get yourself ready.

Inspiration is fine, but inspiration must lead to discipline. It's one thing to be motivated, but it's another thing to be motivated sufficiently to take the classes, do the reading, do the repetition, go through it over and over, until it becomes part of you. And those are challenges. They're not easy, but they're challenges that if you win and develop and grow, that's what determines your place, your return, your equity, the worth you get from the marketplace.

THREE PARTS OF PERSONAL DEVELOPMENT

I've divided personal development into three parts. Let me give you those.

1. Spiritual

I know when you talk spiritual you can get in an argument most anywhere, but I have a simple belief that says humans are not just animals. Some people believe we're just an extension and an advanced form of the animal species, but I believe humans are unique. Spiritual qualities make us different from all other creations. Now I'm an amateur on that side of it, so I can't give you a lot of advice there, but I would recommend you be a student of the spiritual side of your nature. And whatever you have to read and assimilate to develop in that area I would strongly suggest you do.

2. Physical

The mind and the body work together, so we've got to give some attention to both, mind and body. Development of mind and body. On the physical side, you've heard the phrase that says treat your body like a temple. A temple. Not a bad word. Something you would take extremely good care of. Treat your body like a temple, not a woodshed, right? A temple. Take good care of it.

The only house we have to live in currently is the physical body we have and that's part of success in the marketplace. That's physical well-being. It's feeling good about yourself physically, so that you stride into the marketplace with a sense of self-worth, self-confidence, having taken care of that end of it. It covers several parts, including good nutrition. Physically you can do extremely well if you just pay some attention. Read all the books about nutrition to make up your own mind. There are a lot of weird conflicts in the nutritional aspect, but you just have to read and decide for yourself a good plan for you, a good health plan.

Then there's physical appearance. Be skillful enough to take care of your appearance in the marketplace. It has a lot to do with your acceptance. A big share of it is how you appear to other people—on the job, performing, company, community. There's a saying that goes, "God looks on the inside and people look on the outside." That's not a bad suggestion, meaning: Take care of the inside for God, and take care of the outside for people. You say, well, people shouldn't judge you by your appearance. Well, let me tell you, they do! Don't base your life on should and shouldn't. Only base your life on realities. Sure, when people get to know you they'll judge you by more than what they see, but at first they're going to take a look. So, physical appearance is part of the physical side of personal development.

Now, I've got another good phrase for you. It says, be conscious of self, but not self-conscious. There's a certain point that we need to be conscious of ourselves, take care of it, then let it go. Some people worry about their appearance all day and it detracts rather than adds. So take care of it, and then let it go. Do the best you can, and let that get the job done. Be conscious of ourselves, but not to the point of being self-conscious.

3. Mental

Here's the third part to personal development: the mind. Stretching your mind, developing good thinking habits, good study habits, pursuing ideas, and trying to find ways to apply them to human behavior and the marketplace. All of that takes mind-stretch and mind-exercise. Part of it is stretching yourself in reading habits. You can't live on mental candy, so you've got to have the full range of mental food in order to grow. We call that mind-stretch.

Your willingness to tackle subjects that are difficult and that most people have decided to let slide gives you an extraordinary edge in the marketplace. How can you master part of the high skills, the extraordinary skills that make you an unusual performer in the marketplace? It takes mind-stretch. Some people skip poetry and literature, the Bible, history and a lot of things that seem a little difficult to attack. But if you always back away from something that seems a little difficult at first, you leave yourself weak. You leave yourself unprepared in the marketplace. So, don't be afraid to tackle the heavyweight stuff. It may be a lot easier than you think once you get into it and learn skill after skill.

LEARN THE OTHER SIDE OF THE ARGUMENT

Another part of mind-stretch is to learn the other side of the argument. Whether you're debating spiritual, political, physical, behavior, whatever it is, don't be afraid of the other side of the argument. If you're going to be a good debater, you've got to know the other side of the argument. So that's what I'm asking you to do.

Don't be afraid of the other side of the argument. If you're strong mentally, you can handle it, and you've got to give people points for their side of the argument. Give credit to somebody who's got a good point. Even though you don't agree with their argument, you must agree that they came up with a good point. That's part of mind-stretch, studying the other side of the argument.

YOUR PERSONAL DEVELOPMENT LIBRARY

Now part of all this is developing what I call a personal development library. Mr. Shoaff got me started back when I was 25 years old. Since I'd missed most of my college education, he said to me, "I pass it along to you to be self-educated."

Education doesn't cease when you leave college or leave the university. Education is a lifetime process. We keep putting ourselves through the paces to learn. That's how you get into the higher numbers income. That's how you get into the higher brackets enterprise. That's how you become a more useful, productive, valuable citizen, making a contribution to family, community, country, enterprise. Work hard on developing these skills and be self-educated.

Mr. Shoaff said to me, "Standard education gets you standard results." He said why not go beyond the standard and the average and the acceptable and become the advantaged, the extraordinary, or the extra-capable? I picked up on that. I had decided back at age 18 or 19 just to get a job, work hard, and do the best I could. And Mr. Shoaff said there is a lot more to life than that. Why don't you master some extraordinary skills? Why don't you move up to the higher level and see if you wouldn't find the taste better in the results you get from that exercise? I did that.

Now, your personal development library needs to be a whole mix. It can't just be a single piece of it. Some people these days are just into self-improvement, self-help, inspirational things. But you can't live on mental candy alone. You need more than that. Your library needs to be balanced like the pantry in your kitchen. You can't be strong just on the easy stuff. You've got to tackle the full range. We should study history, biographies and autobiographies. Study people who have done unique things, both admirable and despicable. We need to be students of both.

Sometimes novels are great ways of sharing dialogue, ideas and philosophy woven into the story. The sweep of the story carries us along, but sure enough little by little we're getting the dialogue. We need the full range of culture: dance, the arts, literature. Then we need books on geography and language. We need to study a bit of law. No matter what you're going to do in life, we all need a bit of fundamentals on law, contracts, what to sign, what not to sign. Almost everything now has legal implications.

FOUR STEPS TO SUCCESS

I've developed four steps to success in the quest for personal development.

1. Good Ideas

Ideas are the life seeds of enterprise. A better life comes first of all by the search for good ideas. Never cease your quest for knowledge. Finding ideas can be life-changing. Business ideas, social ideas, personal ideas—nothing is as powerful as an idea whose time has come. Be a searcher of good ideas: timely ideas, political ideas, family ideas, ideas for health. Then, do what I do. Keep a journal. Keep a log of good ideas. That's for the serious students. I used to take notes on pieces of paper and found out I couldn't go through them, couldn't catalog them, and I missed a lot of good stuff. So I learned to keep good ideas in a journal and I've been keeping journals all these years. It's an extension of your learning library.

2. Good Plans

Be a student of good plans. Plans are important because they take ideas to the marketplace. Plans give birth to ideas. Plans well executed bring ideas into enterprise and bring ideas into the better life. Ideas without plans forever hang like an artist's rendering on the wall. They never become reality. They never become substance. So, I'm asking you, develop good plans, good disciplined activity plans. Riches do not come by crossing your fingers and walking through the day hoping. Riches and wealth come from well-laid plans.

If a child starts between the ages of 12 and 15 with a good plan and a normal average income, by age 40 they should be wealthy. Age 45 at the latest. Now if you're not wealthy by age 45, it simply means you didn't have a good plan. Opportunity without good plans misses all the worth and wealth you could have. So be a student of good plans.

3. The Passing of Time

All of us have to learn to handle time. It's one of the challenges of life, how to handle the passing of time. Sometimes waiting from spring to fall is difficult to handle. That's not an easy stretch, especially if you have heavyweight creditors. You planted in the spring and now the creditors are on you in the summer. We have a tendency to walk out into the field and say, "Grow crop, grow, they're on me." But we have to learn to wait. Part of success is patience. We Americans probably have to learn patience more than any other people on earth in our push-button society, right? But it takes patience—the passing of time.

4. Solving Problems

The fourth step to success in the quest for personal development is the solving of problems. It's a simple way to describe success. Success is simply solving problems. Now there are all kinds of problems: business problems, family problems, personal problems, financial problems, emotional problems. Everybody's got a list of problems.

Problem solving is where enterprise comes from. This is how you build worth and wealth, solving the problem. I met Neil Armstrong one time, the first man on the moon. He's got a unique talk with his experiences being the first man on the moon. Neil Armstrong put it fairly simply. He said going to the moon and back was simply a matter of solving problems. What a simple way to put it. Problem 1: how to get there. Problem 2: how to get back. That's simple, right? He said make sure you don't leave until you've solved both problems. Well put. Sure, some things are complicated, but if you take it one piece at a time—solve the problems, put it back together—you can't believe the enterprise you can build, the life you can build, the skills you can build. Take it a piece at a time, master it, and then put it back together to solve it.

➤ PUT IT ON PAPER ⮜

Let me give you another tip on solving problems. This was helpful to me. Learn to solve them on paper. I learned this some time ago. You've got to commit some of your thoughts to paper. If you just deal out of your head all the time, it's easy to make too many errors. You wouldn't build a house out of your head.

You take what's in your head, put it on paper and work it out. Then you work from the document. Work from the paper.

First of all, put it on paper. Take a piece of paper and just spend a little time outlining the problem. Instead of just thinking about it, put your thoughts down on paper. Most of the executives I work with around the world use this kind of strategy. Putting a problem on paper. It helps you to focus. It helps you to zero in.

Now when you state the problem to the best of your ability, you just add this one question. Is that all of it? You say, well, we're not to dwell on problems, no, we're not to dwell on them, or live in them, but at least you have got to state them. Because you can't solve them until you clearly define them.

THREE SIMPLE QUESTIONS

Now, let me give you part of the answer to solving problems. Answers to solving problems fall into three simple questions. For problem solving, it's important to go through these questions.

1. What Can I Do?

Here's the first one. What can I do to solve the problem? What can I do? Then you start developing what we call working papers. Working papers simply are doing your best. You say, well, here's potential answer number one. That's an answer. Potential answer number two is a possibility. And number three, that's a possibility. You just start laying out possible solutions. Then go back and analyze these solutions. Number three? You've already come to the conclusion it would take too long. Okay. Number two? Too big a question mark. Number one is probably it. My first inclination was right.

Study that a little more and see if that's it. Develop working papers.

2. What Can I Read?

So the first step to solving problems is to write them down. The second step is to develop working papers on possible solutions, what you can possibly do. Now, if that doesn't do it, here is the second question to ask. What can I read? Sure enough, there may be a book, there may be a text, there may be an audio program, there may be a video, there may be some form of an outline on your particular problem.

If you went to the library, you might find a whole section on your problem. There's bound to be some answers. So now you start going through the books, and start developing your reaction to what you're reading. Just go through all the books, developing your analysis of what you've read. That's the second question. What can I read?

3. Who Can I Ask?

Here's the third question. When solving a problem, who can you ask? Now, here's the key. Don't hesitate to ask. Let me give you the next clue: don't ask first. If you always just ask, usually you don't develop the skills in solving problems. What's more valuable than the solution to a problem? Answer: the skills of solving problems. The skills offer more value than the answer. The answer to a problem is temporary. Skills in solving problems are permanent. So it's not just answers we need. It's skills we need.

› THE FIVE ABILITIES ‹

Learn to concentrate on these five abilities. I call these the five abilities that help you skillfully attack the marketplace to do well.

1. Absorb

Here's the first ability. Develop the ability to absorb, the ability to soak in, take in, be like a sponge. Sitting in class or at the workplace sometimes it's easy to daydream, to be preoccupied, to be somewhere else.

I read a good article once in *Reader's Digest*. The title was, "Wherever You Are, Be There." I thought that was excellent. Be there. Concentration. Sports stars will tell you all you need is just a slight miss of concentration and they put one by your feet and there goes the championship. Just a slight slip of concentration.

Now, it's also important in learning extra skills to really pay attention. Absorb, take in. I have a friend who makes it as exciting when he goes to Acapulco and comes back to tell me about it as it is to go myself. It's unbelievable. Let me tell you why. When he's there, he doesn't miss anything. He soaks it all up. His mind is like a movie projector that takes it all in, the sights, the sounds and the smells and the colors and the people, and what's going on. He sees it all. Then he also has the gift of expression, so when he comes back he can tell you about it, word for word, detail for detail. When he talks, you can feel the water lapping at your feet. You can smell the aroma of the food. You can see the sights and sounds and the colors and the people. I mean, he's got the gift to take it in and then the gift to share it. And those are extremely excellent skills to work on.

Most people are trying to get through the day. I've got a better objective for you. Learn to get from the day. Not just get through it, get from it. Soak it up. Each day is a piece of the mosaic of your life. Don't waste any. Treat it with care. See how much you can get from a day—how much advice, how much information, how much color, how much sight and sound to add to your worth and your wealth and your equity of mind.

2. Respond

Here's the next ability. Develop the skill to respond, the ability to be affected by what you see and hear and sense. Success is not just knowledge. Success is response to knowledge. Success is not just experience. Success is emotion created from experience. It's the emotional part that plays such a major part in our life and our future and our success.

Responding to life means to let sad things make you sad, to let happy things make you happy, to let puzzling things puzzle you. Let things that are difficult create difficulty for you. Respond.

I'm the greatest guy in the world to take to the movies. I get affected by a good movie. I'm willing to go if they want to take me on a good journey. Good movie, good dialogue, something good to see, watch this whole story unfold, I'm willing to go. I forget everything and just go. Be affected by it.

I was in Melbourne, Australia, and I saw an advertisement: "See *Dr. Zhivago* on the Big Screen." I thought, "I've got to go see it on the big screen." They've got these little cracker-box theaters now, right? I like the big movie theaters with the drapes and the chandeliers and the balconies. I mean, that's the movies! These little cracker boxes leave a lot to be desired. But to see a movie in a proper movie theater on a big screen, I got enticed by it, and I'd seen *Dr. Zhivago*, I don't know, probably a half a dozen times. I said, "I've got to go see it one more time on the big screen."

So I go, and sure enough this sweeping saga of the Russian Revolution, *Dr. Zhivago*, unfolds and I'm swept along by it all. But up until that particular time, I had always missed the significance of the end of the movie. This time I got it. The other times I'd missed it.

Comrade General says, "Tanya, how did you come to be lost"? And she says, "I was just lost." He says, "No, how did you come to be lost?" And she didn't want to say. She said, "Well, my father and I were running through the city, it was on fire, the revolution had come and I was lost." And Comrade General said, "No, Tanya, how did you come to be lost?" And she finally said, "While we were running, my father let go of my hand, and I was lost." That's what she didn't want to say. He let go. Comrade General says, "Tanya, that's what I've been trying to tell you. I'm positive Komarovsky was not your real father. This man, Dr. Zhivago, that I knew well, I'm positive he was your father. I've been looking for you. I think I found you." And he said, "Tanya, let me tell you something, if this man, your real father, had been there, he would never have let go of your hand."

And I got it—I got it that time! Wow. The other times I'd missed it. I'm eating popcorn waiting for the movie to finish the other times, I guess. So that's what I'm asking you to do. I'm asking you to get it, and I'm asking you to let it affect you, let it do things to you. It builds your emotional bank.

3. Reflect

The third ability: Learn to reflect. Reflecting is an extra way of getting more value from what you know and what you've been through. Reflecting is going back over.

Let me give you some good times to reflect. Take just a few minutes at the end of the day and go back over the day. Find a place, if you can, to be alone, and just go back and think through the day. Where have you been? What did you see? What did you hear? What did you feel? If you'll just relive it, go back through it, I'm telling you it will add multiplied value to you. The day you've just been through will be more valuable for your future if you just go back through it.

Take a few hours at the end of the week. Take hours at the end of the week, and minutes at the end of the day. Take hours at the end of the week, half a day at the end of the month, and a weekend at the end of the year. Those are called times to reflect. Now, why go back over, why run the tapes again? Let me tell you why, to make the past more valuable.

It's like color enhancers. The camera takes pictures of Jupiter on its flyby, but let me tell you what they do with those pictures. The computer has learned to enhance them with color so that they become vivid and unique and our eyes get big and we take a look and we say, wow. That's what will happen with your life. If you'll take the time to review what's going on, review the decision-making, review the people you're with, review the actions you're taking, the decisions you're making, review all that stuff, go back through the feeling, I'm telling you, the color enhancers of your own mind will make your life more valuable.

Now, why try to make your life valuable? Simple answer: to invest it in the future. We call that bright. We call that skillful, to make more out of your past, to have more value to invest in the future, instead of just trying to get through one more day, trying to get through one more week. It's to get more out of your past and invest it in your future. When my father was about to turn 76, I said, "Dear father of mine, can you imagine how exciting it's going to be to take the last 75 years of your life and invest them in your 76th?" That's an extraordinary thing to learn, how to take more of you and invest it in the next conversation, invest it in the next decision, invest it in the next activity.

4. Act

Now, here's number four. Develop the ability to act, the ability to take action on your feelings and your knowledge. Disciplined action is what gives birth to ideas, enterprise and values. Without activity, ideas and dreams have no life.

Disciplined activity is the most demanding of arts to take you where you want to go. Now, sometimes it doesn't take much of a change of activity. Daily or weekly disciplines are those small changes of intelligent activity that take you in a better direction.

Here's a good way to look at it. Ten years from now you will surely arrive. The question is, where? Now is the time to fix the next 10 years. Fix a better course. Now, to unsophisticated people, what they do during the day doesn't seem to matter. But to sophisticated people, it makes all the difference in the world. The books you read, the actions you take, the disciplines you engage in on a daily basis, those are the activities that are taking you somewhere, and all of us need to take a look at where our daily activities are taking us.

The activity of learning, the activity of mind, health disciplines, wealth disciplines, culture disciplines, all values come from disciplines. Ideas put into disciplined activity create value.

5. Share

The fifth ability in our personal development quest for skills that create success in the marketplace is the ability to share. Sharing is a unique human capacity. Sharing is a phenomenon, especially in the human experience. It seems when we share we are the bigger and better for it.

It seems like if you share something and give it away, you'd have less. But it's a paradox. What you share creates more for you. That's why we call it a paradox. You're not diminished by sharing. You're increased.

If you have a child and you love it dearly, and if a second child comes along must you now cut your love in half? The answer is no. From some strange, mysterious source comes an increased capacity. From sharing with the first, capacity and an awareness and uniqueness are increased. So that is what I would ask you to do, become gifted in sharing.

There are many ways to share. One is by language, the gift of language. One of the most important studies for you is the study of communication, how to affect other people with words.

➤ HAVE SOMETHING GOOD TO SAY ➤

Here are some steps toward sharing with good communication. Have something good to say. You can't speak what you don't know. Talking is like writing a check. You want to make sure you've got a verbal check that will cash when you get ready to talk. And here's the true power of communication. When what you say is only the tip of the iceberg of what you know. We call that power. I'm sure we've all been around people who quickly told us more than they knew. Do your homework. Have something good to share. Have something good to say. Communication is part of sharing.

➤ SAY IT WELL ➤

Part of the gift of language is saying it uniquely. Winston Churchill had the unique ability to take the English language and send it into battle. The words he composed and the speeches he gave and the language and style gave such hope and uniqueness and structure to the free world that soon the enemy was defeated. But part of it was the structure of the language, the skill, the gift of saying things well. It is one of those incredible skills, saying it well.

➤ READ YOUR AUDIENCE ◄

When you talk, you've just got to be interested enough to look and see how you're doing. Learn to read your audience. I had to learn that. At first, I was so absorbed in what I was saying that I'm sure the audience could have left and I would have never known it. But I finally learned to look up to see what's going on here, over here, in the back. That was an experience for me, learning to read, to see, to study the reflection of whoever you're communicating with. That's an art, a skill.

› SAY IT WITH INTENSITY ‹

Words with strong feeling behind them change the meaning. Words can have power if they're loaded with emotion and belief, courage, love, understanding, awareness, sympathy, concern, being touched by somebody. If you put more of that into what you say, it'll have an incredible effect.

So share your knowledge. You can't believe how well you can help somebody just by recommending a book. Recommend a poem. Share a word, a phrase. You say, "Hey, I just read this, and I think you'll get a lot out of it." Somebody reads it and comes back and says, "Hey, that had an impact on my life, and I'm glad you shared that with me." Then you start getting compliments.

It's an incredible feeling when people tell you, "What you said made a difference for me." But you don't have to lecture in front of thousands of people to get that same feedback. All you have to do is recommend a book or share an idea. Somebody comes back and says, "That book got me started," or "The things you told me at breakfast that morning, wow, I've been thinking about that and I'm making some changes." You can experience this incredible pleasure that comes from sharing ideas.

Remember, what you pour out creates a capacity for more. So pour out what you know. Pour out what you feel. Let go in a sharing way the good things that have come your way. That's a major part of the skill in the marketplace of developing success, wealth and value.

› THE PERSON YOU WISH TO BECOME ‹

So, develop skills that make you attractive to the marketplace. Develop the temperament and the attitude that make you attractive to the business world, the attitude and the temperament that make you a splendid husband, wife, father, mother, son, daughter, friend, coworker, business partner. Because, here's what's important: it's not what you get that makes you valuable, it's what you become that makes you valuable.

One last phrase to consider in the quest for personal development: Promise is on the other side of price. For the promise, you must always pay the price. If you want the glory of success, the glory of a unique family, the glory and the recognition of a unique enterprise, the glory of a job well done, then you've got to pay upfront. And the discipline of developing skills for the marketplace is part of the pay. But once you get a taste of value, you don't mind paying the discipline. I wish for you all these good things that come from paying the price.

THE JIM ROHN GUIDE SERIES

The timeless wisdom of Jim Rohn in concise, easy-to-read guides. Perfect for sharing with friends, family, business associates, clients and prospects.

TIME MANAGEMENT
PERSONAL DEVELOPMENT
LEADERSHIP
GOAL SETTING
COMMUNICATION

Quantity discounts available
JimRohn.com or
store.SUCCESS.com